Start Your Day Right

Coffee And Jesus

By Lisa Banados

Note To My Readers,

Good days start with a hot fresh cup of coffee, and with Jesus! Nowadays in the day that you live in, you are going to have to get your strength from something, and that should be from Jesus. He will strengthen you for your days ahead, and will help to equip you for your journey!

Dedication

To all those that show up each, and every day to do life, and want more, and not merely just coast through life keep on reading!

Acknowledgments

I acknowledge my Lord of which none of this could have ever been possible! I want to take the time, and to tell you thank you for all that you have done, and continue to do in my life, and the life of my family!

Introduction

How many of you are struggling with the grind, and with the day-to-day life? How many of you are exhausted by the end of the day, only to get up, and do the whole thing all over again?

How long do you think you could put up with it? How long do you think you could keep a good attitude? How long can you keep this up? The grind is considered dreary, monotonous, or difficult labor, study, or routine, like the grind at the office, or work.

With all of that going on we are going to have to do better with taking care of one another, and helping each other out! When you are better able to do that then life as you know it will change, and change for those around you too!

How about being more like the Good Samaritan in the word of God where there was a man that was walking down the street, and he was robbed, beaten, they stripped him of his clothing, and they just left him!

There were several individuals that just walked on by, and acted like they didn't see him. Nobody was willing to take time out of their day, and show some kindness! What if you were to flip that script, and not just pass on by when you see someone in need? How about being there for someone that needs you?

How about getting yourself out of the judgment seat, and just give a helping hand? How about raising the bar, and being a part of the change that is needed in this world?

If everyone were to do part that they are suppose to then perhaps, the daily grind wouldn't be so arduous. Maybe, just maybe it would help for someone to feel like the daily grind is doable! Within these pages you will find compelling inspiration, and encouragement, that will ultimately help you to come up in life, and reign the way the Lord has intended!

Table Of Contents

Chapter 1

Not My Problem

Have you ever asked your children to go clean up some dishes or to throw the bottles of water in the garbage and they will say that it isn't their dishes, or it wasn't their bottle? Another words they were ultimately saying it wasn't their problem so why should they bother!

Well the Good Samaritan could of had the same attitude, which a good amount of the world has (as you could see, and experience sometimes), that no one wanted to take the time, and help the one that was on the side of the road, and was beat down!

They wanted to do like some of the people in New York are viewed as in the movie Spider Verse when Miles and the other Spider-Man were laying on the ground, and they were literally walking all over them trying to get past them, and they couldn't do it fast enough.

No one in that particular movie bent down, and offered to help them either. In the movie "Mortgage Apple Cakes" Angela Logan was having some issues with keeping her house, but she didn't want to burden anybody with her troubles. She didn't think that anybody would want to help her out, but she was wrong!

Kimberly Elise, which plays Angela Logan who was a single mom with three sons and a broke down home! Well she had ten days to go, and save her home. She gets inspired to sell one hundred apple cakes, at forty dollars each to save their home! Little did she know that everything would take off the way it did.

Not only did they save their home, but have a budding, and thriving business to go along with it. In the movie she talks about soup, and how basically we should be helping each other out. She had the mindset that others may have what they need!

She says they may not have all the ingredients that they need to make a soup, but someone they know would probably have a potato, someone else may have a carrot, and so on. Since she had that mindset initially even though their family was basically poor, she had the foundation of which to build, and she taught her children that too.

With that mentality she has amassed a business, that is worldwide! When I think about things like this I wonder what happened to the freedom to be able to go to your neighbor, and ask for some sugar or eggs? We had that with the neighbors that we were living next to for about five years, and then they moved. They were so friendly, introduced themselves, and were so congenial! We even did coffee mornings together!

Nowadays, it is like every man for themselves, and survival of the fittest, but how many are really surviving the economic system that you now have in the world? With the gas prices that were soaring, and everything else for that matter, I mean people were struggling! Just to buy some eggs you had to take a collection from the family to go out, and get some eggs that were five dollars, and if your family had any size to it, those eggs wouldn't last long!

The struggle can be real y'all! We have got to take better care of those around us, and do our best to pay attention!

It's just like in the movie "Samaritan" where Sylvester Stallone plays Mr. Smith the superhero that has super sonic strength, a recluse who was a garbage man, that had basically gone underground, and doesn't want to be bothered!

He pays attention to the bullying that this thirteen-year-old named Sam Clery is going through. Sam discovers Mr. Smith in the neighborhood, and begins to seek him out!

The Samaritan was well known but nobody had seen or heard of him for many years, so when Sam was trying to let others know they didn't believe him. Well Sam was having issues with bullies, and the Samaritan was the only one that cared, and helped out this kid. This reminds me of the Good Samaritan in the word of God! Let's take a look!

But a Samaritan (foreigner), who was traveling, came upon him; and when he saw him, he was deeply moved with compassion [for him], Luke 10:33 Amp.

All you have to do is to show compassion, and the world all around you would catch the flame, it would spread, and we could all help each other through the daily grind!

Jesus replied, "A man was going down from Jerusalem to Jericho, and he encountered robbers, who stripped him of his clothes [and belongings], beat him, and went their way [unconcerned], leaving him half dead. Luke 10:30 Amp.

Now by coincidence a priest was going down that road, and when he saw him, he passed by on the other side. Luke 10:31 Amp.

We as people need to quit passing other people when we know they are in need, and see if we could help them out some way!

Likewise a Levite also came down to the place and saw him, and passed by on the other side [of the road]. Luke 10:32 Amp.

and went to him and bandaged up his wounds, pouring oil and wine on them [to sooth and disinfect the injuries]; and he put him on his own pack-animal, and brought him to an inn and took care of him. Luke 10:34 Amp.

On the next day he took out two denarii (two days' wages) and gave them to the innkeeper, and said, 'Take care of him; and whatever more you spend, I will repay you when I return.' Luke 10:35 Amp.

Wow what an example of what Jesus would do, and how He would handle such a thing!

Which of these three do you think proved himself a neighbor to the man who encountered the robbers?" Luke 10:36 Amp.

He answered, "The one who showed compassion and mercy to him." Then Jesus said to him, "Go and constantly do the same." Luke 10:37 Amp.

The Lord wants you to do the same, as what the Good Samaritan had done. Just go, and have compassion for others, go, and care for others, Just go, and see what you could do for somebody else, just go, and lend a helping hand.

Don't just dodge people, and be concerned about yourself only. Yes, there is self-care, and you definitely need to do that, but just because you do self-care doesn't mean that it is solely all about you. I am so serious right now!

There is such an issue in America with this that I'm talking with the daily grind, and how people are barely making it in their mentalities, and are stressed to the max, and having issues in their body because they are dealing with so much, and when you are dealing with things so much, and you don't have any relief then they are getting stretched way beyond their own capacities, and their health is a clear reflection of that!

When there is such a great problem to this degree in the world, we cannot ignore it. We cannot keep putting on these band-Aids that are only temporary because my friends this is not working, and the world at large is getting sick, but at the same time we could turn this thing if only you would reach down, and help one other person come up.

Ask them how they are doing! Ask them do they need anything. Ask them if there is anything that you could pray for them about! You might be surprised as to what answer you may get, because I have talked to many people, and each one had said that they were dealing with something.

Some it was financial issues, and others it was health issues! If you were to do a concensus of those around you l, and you were to ask them those questions I just gave you, what answers would they give you if they were completely honest? What would they say?

Oh, and when you ask those questions be sure, and wait for the answer, and when they say something do your best to go ahead, and respond the best way that you know!

Don't be afraid of what the possible response may be. You may not be able to fully help in the area of which they may have a need in, but maybe you know of someone that could, and you could refer them to someone that could help!

If the person that you thought could help isn't able to then keep on till you find someone that could help to bring them some relief.

Carry one another's burdens and in this way you will fulfill the requirements of the law of Christ [that is, the law of Christian love]. Galatians 6:2 Amp.

This is something that you are supposed to do whether your plate is too full, or not! I mean if you think about it what if everyone's plate was too full, and didn't have the extra time to help?

Maybe that is some of the issues with the world right now! Everyone just seems like they are too busy, let alone have time to care! With all that Jesus was doing, He still had time to come through, and heal the sick, set people free, deliver people, and a myriad of other things!

If Jesus had the time to do so, certainly you, and I could carve some time out in our day to give a helping hand, or to make a phone call, or to text someone!

This is My commandment, that you love and unselfishly seek the best for one another, just as I have loved you. John 15:12 Amp.

There are many ways to express how you love someone! I understand when there is so many people that are barely getting by, and their daily grind. I totally get it!

Each day can prove to be eventful for many people in any given day, let alone any given week. It is what you do in those moments that will determine if you stay there in the chaos, or can move past it on to better, and greater things!

The reason for me writing this book is due to hearing all of what is going on in the world, and even abroad!

There are so many people that are crying out for help, and many aren't sure how to ask for help, let alone get the actual help that they need. Some people are feeling helpless to degree because they aren't able to help people out the way they want to. Well I would say to that to just do what you can with what you have.

Eventually your resources will increase, and you will be able to do even more! When I sat, and watched "Ice Roads" with Liam Neeson there was some coal miners that were trapped underground, and there wasn't anyone that was able to help them out right offhand!

They had to rely on the truckers that had to go over some ice roads, with some heavy eighteen-wheelers, that were carrying the machinery that they needed in order to free the guys that were in the mine.

There were only three drivers, three trucks, in the month of April. It is in the month of March is when they quit going across the ice roads, because by April it was starting to warm up.

It wasn't necessarily the pick of the liter with the drivers, because the drivers usually go to Hawaii or some place like that when it was the off season.

They had one that was really experienced, they had another one that was little bit experienced, but couldn't really hold a job because he had some issues, and the other driver was a young person. This reminds of the disciples that Jesus rolled with, and how they weren't necessarily the upper echelon.

You see the Lord looks at the heart, and He does look on the outside! Well these miners were waiting on these three drivers, a mechanic, and someone that was posing to be someone he was not.

Well one of the miners got a response as to how long it would take for the truck drivers to come, and get them out. It said ASAP. One of the other miners had said what do they mean by ASAP.

Do they mean six hours, twelve hours, or thirty hours. ASAP to me means right away. However those truck drivers were way far away, and it was probably going to take even more then thirty hours. When your friends say they are going to help, and you need it immediately what does ASAP means for them.

Hopefully ASAP to them doesn't mean six hours, twelve hours, or even thirty hours. However keep in mind people have lives, and they have a whole lot going on themselves.

They most likely have a spouse, might have some children, and a life to put on hold (of which I'm sure they don't mind) but please keep in mind they will be there as soon as they can.

You don't know what kind of obstacles they are having to scale in the process of getting to you to help you! Just like in the movie "Ice Roads," the truckers had gone through so many obstacles on their way to help these coal miners that were stuck under ground!

Their gas line was cut, hijacked, beaten, and threatened! Yet they were on their way! It may not be to that degree with your family, or friends when they respond, but just know they very well may have to go through something to get to you, and help you out.

Just wanted to provide some understanding for those moments when you need someone to respond to a need of yours, and it doesn't happen as quickly as you would like it to! If everyone were to have the mentality that whatever problems, situations, or issues someone may have, and to think of isn't your problem isn't healthy.

You'll have to change your mentality with that, because in the world that you live in you don't want to walk around thinking like that.

If everyone were to seriously have that mentality thinking that someone else was going to help someone, rather then helping themselves then that is literally passing the buck. You don't want to pass the buck, because if it is in your hands to do it then you should do it. Don't expect someone else to do what you are supposed to do!

Or what man is there among you who, if his son asks for bread, will [instead] give him a stone? Luke 7:9 Amp.

I really do my best when someone asks for something that I give them what they need!

Or if he asks for a fish, will [instead] give him a snake? Luke 7:10 Amp.

If you then, evil (sinful by nature) as you are, know how to give good and advantageous gifts to your children, how much more will your Father who is in heaven [perfect as He is] give what is good and advantageous to those who keep on asking Him. Matthew 7:11 Amp.

Let's say you jump at the chance to be able to help someone out, and help them along with the daily grind. When you lighten their load, I know the Lord will send someone to lighten your load, and we will all be the better for it!

Time To Reflect

1. What are some of the things that you have been passing the buck on?

Time To Reflect

2.How can you exhibit the character of the Good Samaritan?

Chapter 2

Permission

You don't have to ask for permission to take a break when you think you are in need of one! Sure you may have to be creative about coordinating with someone or schedule yourself in for some time off on your own calendar, but you sure don't have to ask for permission!

Whoever said that you need to ask for permission to pamper yourself, or to treat yourself? Treating yourself doesn't have to be expensive it could be the simple thing as sneaking in a nap, when the house is all a buzz with everyone running around doing what they are doing.

I had recently had done that even though everyone was home, and I just felt like leaning back in the recliner, and treating myself to a good nap so I did! I wasn't necessarily expecting everyone to tiptoe around me, but I figured I would just get a quick short nap in, and when everything settled I would wake up and be even more ready for the rest of the day!

Only the Lord knows what a day holds, but I know in whom holds the day! My Lord knows exactly what will transpire in a day, and I was feeling like taking a nap so I took one. I didn't ask anyone for permission, or see what else was going on for the day I just sat back relaxed, and went to sleep.

I woke up refreshed, renewed, and glad I took a nap. Interesting enough when I took a nap everyone in the house just went about doing what they do, and the rest of the evening was a beautiful one indeed! So when you want to do a simple thing as to take a nap, but maybe you have some younger children why not slide in when they are taking their naps.

It's a win-win situation! Some days may be easier then others to get in a nap. Maybe your thing is taking a hot bath, or something else for that matter. Whatever it is for you be sure, and get it in the best way you know how. You may have to ask your spouse to take over for the children for an hour or so.

From the days of John the Baptist until now the kingdom of heaven suffers violent assault, and violent men seize it by force [as a precious prize] Matthew 11:12 Amp.

There are some things that you ask for for permission, and taking care of yourself shouldn't be one of them. I am merely emphasizing this point because it seems like the world around you, and at large is hemorrhaging.

It also seems like it is coming apart at the seams. Getting back to the basics of taking care of oneself first, and then moving on to others is imperative if you are going to make things work. Picture it this way you make up a "To Do List" today, and you put every single thing on it from day to day, and you are never at the top.

You are taking care of your pup more then you are taking care of yourself. You are working twelve hour shifts (to help cover the bills) your running your children to school, to soccer practice, to ballet lessons, piano lessons, birthday parties on the weekend, buying groceries for the household, buying gas, going to the Post Office, buying flowers, buying clothes for everyone in the house but you, taking your children to eye appointments, taking your children to get their haircuts, taking your children to the doctor's appointment, going to the bank, taking your children to the park, taking your children to their friend's house, your doing piles of laundry (that seems like it never ends) washing the car, your doing loads of dishes, (that doesn't seem like it is going to quit any time soon),taking your children to dental appointments, and a myriad other things!

You do this day to day, with not even putting yourself on the list you are going to wear out quickly, and your family is going to wonder what had happened to you, because you took that super woman off the front of your chest, and put away your red cape, and your red high heel boots, and finally said enough is enough! I give you permission to flip that script!

I give you permission to live your life, and to enjoy it! Sure you could do all of those things, but take a few minutes in the morning with the Lord, take a few moments for yourself, finish that cup of coffee, do a devotional or something, and gather yourself before you literally go, and take on the world!

It may sound like some strong words, but when you take a moment, and really think about all of what you do in a day you could most certainly wear a super woman suit, and could probably identify with Wonder Woman! Reminder Wonder Woman was a super hero to the people. Perhaps you focus on God first, and foremost. Next it should be on your spouse, children, and family as a whole!

I know that there is nothing better for them than to rejoice and to do good as long as they live; Ecclesiastes 3:12 Amp.

and also that every man should eat and drink and see and enjoy the good of all his labor—it is the gift of God. Ecclesiastes 3:13 Amp.

The Lord will give you the strength, and the power to enjoy everything that the Lord has given you! Always recognize what the Lord is doing in your life, and you will always be blessed because you did!

Strength and dignity are her clothing and her position is strong and secure; And she smiles at the future [knowing that she and her family are prepared]. Proverbs 31:25 Amp.

I was listening to K-LOVE one morning, and it was talking about how bullying looks in many different forms.

Of course you have children bullying other children on the playground! You have the bully at work, that wants to make you feel like they have everything together but they don't.

Then you have the indirect bully that wants to exclude children on the playground, and not include them in the playground activities. Or how about the indirect bullying where children exclude other children at the cafeteria, and don't want to sit with them.

Well they were talking about why not invite the kid over to where you are sitting. How about in the lunchroom at work why not invite them over to where you are sitting, and strike up a conversation!

You never know what a simple boost to their confidence that alone would be. Invite people out of their loneliness, and give them some warm company. How would Jesus want you to handle it?

I still try, and ask myself this same question! It's so important to do this every so often, because there is going to be time periods where you are going to ask for wisdom in certain situations, and it is important when you get some answers to adhere to what you are being told.

There is nothing wrong with asking for help when you actually think that you need some help. The Lord will most assuredly help you along with what you are dealing with!

The thing is you have to continue to look up from where your help comes from. Your help will only come from Him, and it will sometimes filter down through people around you! There is nothing wrong with utilizing those friendships, and family, and what not. We are to bear ye one another's burdens!

There may be times that you have to pitch hit for someone, and stand in proxy for someone, and to help them out. You still don't have to ask for permission to enjoy yourself in the process of it all. I mean why not?

Some of the roads along the way to help someone out may be a bit rough, but you could take it. When you sow into someone's life, you never know how it could change things!

Yes, you could literally help to change someone's life for the better by being kind to them. When you throw around kindness like confetti, you are helping to bring in some happy moments to them as well. Who doesn't want to help bring in some happy!

Nowadays appreciation is wearing pretty thin with those around you, and abroad. Some people are barely making it through, let alone making it through with some appreciation, or thankfulness. You never know what a person is working through, or what kind of storm is trying to rage against them.

It is so imperative that you take the time, and appreciate those that are around you. Appreciate those of which the Lord has put in your life. Appreciate the gifts that are inside people, and encourage their gifts to be used, and to come out, and to flourish.

Encourage the gift of God that may reside in them so deeply. Maybe the cares of the world is tried to snuff out that gift, and trying to make it dormant.

Just maybe the enemy is trying to bring these storms so often to where they are doing their best to stay afloat, let alone make it to the other side to discover, of God's goodness, and blessings in their life!

That is the whole point of the enemy's attacks is to distract you ultimately from what the Lord is doing in your life, and in the lives of your loved ones as well!

And He got up and [sternly] rebuked the wind and said to the sea, "Hush, be still (muzzled)!" And the wind died down [as if it had grown weary] and there was [at once] a great calm [a perfect peacefulness]. Mark 4:39 Amp.

When Jesus rebukes the wind, everything that had previously been standing up has to sit down! Anything that has been out of alignment, or anything that was outside the lines of where a person should be would have to straighten up, and get right.

That is the thing about your Lord Jesus when He speaks to something it has to obey. It isn't an option, it isn't a suggestion, it isn't something that may happen in the near future no it is something that has to happen immediately!

When you know this you will exemplify, and mirror exactly that. It may take some time though, because things don't just happen over night. It takes some time. You know right? That is quite alright for you to have to take some time before you get it down pat real good.

The good thing in life you have to work towards. Nothing is going to be given to you on a platter, nor will you be given a silver spoon. Working towards something good in life is going to take some hard work, and you will definitely appreciate that even more in life.

When you receive something too easily in life you most likely wouldn't enjoy it as much as when you did by when you had to go through several storms along the way so the Lord could ultimately prove the contents of your heart! It is imperative to get to the point to where rather then just go ahead, and assuming that you could do something to just go ahead, and get with the Lord in prayer, and simply just ask!

When you are able to master the art of asking you have truly come up to a whole notha level! I'm not saying that it is going to be the easiest thing to do initially if you are use to doing things without asking, but it will get easier because you have learned a new habit, and a whole new way of doing, and going about things according to the word of God!

As iron sharpens iron, So one man sharpens [and influences] another [through discussion]. Proverbs 27:17 Amp.

Being around other people that put the Lord first in their lives, adhere to the word of God, and do their best to walk it out day in, and day out then you are bound to be in a position to have iron that sharpens iron. You are just basically helping each other to be a sharpener tool in the Lord's tool shed. The Lord has different vessels to do certain things, and to accomplish the will of God for their lives.

Now in a large house there are not only vessels and objects of gold and silver, but also vessels and objects of wood and earthenware, and some are for honorable (noble, good) use and some for dishonorable (ignoble, common). 2 Timothy 2;20 Amp.

Therefore if anyone cleanses himself from these things [which are dishonorable-disobedient, sinful}, he will latter, he will be a vessel for honor, sanctified [set apart for a special purpose], useful to the Master, prepared for every good work. 2 Timothy 2:21 Amp.

Being a vessel of honor, and making choices daily that will help you to ultimately be a vessel of honor is something in which not everyone is going to be cheering you on twenty-four seven, all day, every day! Just know that everything is going according to His master plan!

Perhaps the Lord are wanting you to focus more on Him, and not on the distractions that may be trying to get your attention. The distractions are going to always be there. There really isn't any way to get around that. However you could get to the place to where your focus could get so strong, that the distractions no longer bother you!

Even though it may seem like it gets thick some times, just know that the Lord has equipped, empowered, and given you everything you will ever need to overcome anything that you may encounter! The Lord has already made a way out of no way, and will continue to prosper you, and propel you into your new chapter!

There are some new plains, and there are some new horizons that are ready to be discovered! You will eventually learn how to weather the different elements that are sometimes associated with the storms that you may have in life.

Thinking on your toes will be a normal thing, and it won't get you all bent out of shape to do it, because you are growing, still learning, and following every lead of the Lord. When you encounter the elements it is important for you, and those around you to keep their cool.

Not everyone is going to be able to do it, unless you learn to totally rely, and depend on the Lord. He knows how to get you through, He knows how to navigate, He knows where to take you even though your visibility is hampered with all of the various elements that are associated with progress, being elevated, and success!

It is imperative that the weight of everything in your life is evenly distributed, and that you have and maintain a balance.

You don't have to ask permission for what to put on your plate or platter. You will know what you have been graced for, and what you haven't been graced for! You will most assured know because the Lord will show you, and direct you along the way!

Be sure, and follow His direction, and you'll be sure to come up in life, and have the life that Jesus died on the cross for.

No longer shall you be asking for permission to have a good life, no longer should you ask permission for abundance, no longer shall you ask permission to enjoy the fruits of your labor, no longer shall you ask permission to have your cabinets full of food, no longer shall you ask permission to have a full tank of gas, no longer shall you ask permission to have that dream of a grand house that you are believing for. The Lord is not holding out on you, and He doesn't withhold any good thing from those that who walk uprightly before Him!

For the Lord God is a sun and shield; The Lord bestows grace and favor and honor; No good thing will He withhold from those who walk uprightly. Psalm 84:11 Amp.

Be sure and know that you don't have to ask permission to enjoy the goodness of God! With having the daily grind it is important to realize, and know that you need to start every day with Jesus! This reminds me of a pillow that I have, and it says

"Good days start with coffee, and Jesus." This is a constant reminder of how important it is to start each day with Jesus, and it is also imperative to have continued progress in life! It is important to have, and maintain the mentality Jesus over everything! So He could help you live a life well played!

Time To Reflect

1.Why do you think it is so important to ask permission?

Time To Reflect

2. Be sure, and make it a habit to never assume anything and to ask permission. What are some of the ways of doing so?

Chapter 3

Kick Start

There are many ways to kick start your morning! Some people drink coffee, some people drink tea, some people drink juice, some have smoothies, and some have water with lemons. Whatever you choose to drink in the mornings to get your day kick started it is totally up to you. Just be sure, and to start your day with your Lord, and the trajectory of your life will totally change!

When you allow the Lord to kick start your life, even if you need to start all over again He could still set you on high, and you could still have great success! All you have to do is believe long enough, and keep believing until the full manifestation of it happens!

Until then just stay in faith, and keep feeding the flame of faith, and the flame of doubt will be drowned out! It may sound like it is easier said then done, but it is definitely doable you just have to hold on, know that your help is soon to be coming! Until then keep your lamp lit, and shine brightly so that it makes the darkness in your life dissipate, and be no more!

Maybe you have had a hard life, perhaps you have had a difficult life, just maybe you didn't grow up on the right side of tracks, or perhaps you didn't get that degree you wanted to get, well I have good news for you none of that really matters when it comes to the kingdom of God. After all, He is about the heart, and not about all that other stuff.

He doesn't disqualify you just because you aren't a pedigree. When the Lord puts His hands on you none of that matters. What matters is the call of God on your life, and you answering it!

The Lord will equip you with every single thing that you would ever need for it! It may not show up altogether when you may think, however just know that everything is time released, and will show up exactly when it is needed, and when you need to utilize it. Until then just stay chill, and enjoy the goodness of God that surrounds you on a daily basis!

Enjoying the good life that the Lord has blessed you with is His reward that He gives! There are many people that are making a whole lot of money, but they don't have the power to enjoy what they have. There are some very unhappy people out there.

They may not understand as to why they aren't very happy, but perhaps the answer is deeper than what they were thinking. It is important to take your pit stops along the way, just like what you would see with Daytona!

They have to do so many laps around a track, and then they have to come in for a pit stop to where they get their tires changed, they could get some water, gas up, and continue to get on down the road! It is those pit stops that allow for the driver whoever they may be to be able to continue to make continued progress, continued forward movement, and ultimately success in life overall!

I mean isn't this apart of why you wake up in the morning, and do what you do? It is important to figure out what your why is. Why do you wake up in the morning, and go to work?

Why do you get up in the morning, and take those College courses that you wanted so long to take? Why do you care so much about the community, and the world at large to want to make a difference?

Why do you want to do what you want to do? Retracing your why as to the different things that you would want to accomplish is important! When you do this it will be easier for you to stay on track when those distractions try to hinder you.

When distractions start to try, and hinder you don't let it bother you it is all a part of the progress to go forward, and to continue to succeed. A kick start doesn't have to be some type of loud roar either. I remember years ago, when I had a moped, and it was yellow. I had so much fun on that thing. It had a kick start, and that was exactly what I needed to get me on down the road.

Don't worry about what the Lord may use to get you there, as long as you are willing, and obedient you shall eat the good, and fat of the land!

If you are willing and obedient, You shall eat the best of the land; Isaiah 1:19 Amp.

As long as you choose to be willing, and obedient there isn't anything that could stop you, and you literally become unstoppable as long as you follow every leading of the Lord.

This isn't something that happens over night, but it is a process of which the Lord will work with you, and see you through to the other side. There is nothing to be afraid of even though it may be scary at times. You just feel the fear, adjust and carry on!

Once you move on from there it is then the Lord will start sending you some of the things that you had been praying for for a long time! You just have to learn the art of waiting. There is a saying that "good things come to those that wait."

Well then that is just letting you know that sometimes you just have to wait for the good stuff! When you wait long enough for the good stuff to come in, that waiting will help you to keep, and maintain all the good things that the Lord has in store for you!

The world wants things quickly, and hardly anybody ever wants to wait. People want fast food, their snacks, and some money so they could purchase those items that they may have had to put off from buying because things cost money, and the price of things has recently gone up.

I enjoy going to "Sam's Club" because you could pick up all your essentials, and then you could go in there, and find some fun stuff too! You could buy so much stuff in bulk like your toilet tissue, paper towels, and napkins.

Then you could grab you some snacks. The snack sizes are so big, but they don't really cost that much. So when we buy things from there initially we may spend some money, but it sure does last a whole lot longer then what we were thinking it would last! We buy a lot of toilet tissue when it comes to restocking it! We try, and stay ahead of that.

The reason behind shopping at "Sam's Club" would be to purchase items according to the needs of your family, and proceed to shop according! The store is so big, and everything is pretty much bulk, it takes a lot of discipline to not want to buy everything!

Having some type of budget has a great way to be able to handle the vast choices that "Sam's Club" offers. Also having in place a spending budget that you will need before you enter the door is so very important!

That will help you to hurdle the temptation of overspending, anything, and everything in life! That is applicable in many areas, and that is something that you could take to the bank!

When you do that often enough it will help you to successfully navigate through those tough times. You will successfully navigate successfully through issues, problems, situation, and those things the enemy would try to use to trip you up.

It is always a good thing to stay up on your reading of the newspaper, watching some CNN or some kind of broadcast that the Lord may give you to help keep you in the mix! Utilizing the news broadcast in your local area, even catching the updates on your phone will help you to stay in the know!

When you know what the contents of your daily newspaper is, with watching CNN and all that then you will know, see, and understand what is going on in the world around you! This is so vital living in the day, and age that you are in!

This would only help you to know what you need to be focused on with school closures, how to dress your children, grandchildren, and know how you would need to step out the front door!

Nowadays they are having widespread power outages, and whatnot so it would behoove you to know what is going on around you, and you could do all this while sitting down, and having your favorite cup of Joe, or your favorite cup of tea! Being educated in the things around you may take some time, and you may need to carve out some time in your life to do so!

Getting a good start to your day will help to steer, and chart your day altogether! When you take the time to set up the night before, and get your coffee prepared, prepare your clothes for the next day, prepare your children's clothes for the next day, and meal prep, figure out what meal you are going to have the next day, have an idea of what is in the refrigerator, or what is not for when you make that jaunt to the grocery store, and whatever else it is the night before that will help you to have a good kick start the next day, be sure, and take the time to get yourself all prepared, and ready to go!

If you are already prepared for the day, then you won't have to get ready for the day! The kick start my friend has already begun!

Time To Reflect

1. Jot down some of the ways to kick start your day!

2. What kind of breakfast do you have in order to kick start your day?

Chapter 5

Take Breaks

If you don't take the proper breaks along the way you aren't really helping yourself out at all. You have to do self-care! I can't say that enough! When you are cooking, cleaning, loading the dishwasher, downloading the dishwasher, doing laundry, folding laundry, putting away the laundry, vacuuming, sweeping, dusting, watering the plants, watering the lawn, washing the car you have to get your breaks in!

The movie "Glory Road" it's about a coach Don Haskins (Josh Lucas) that decides to choose talent rather then race. It was about a basketball team and they were going for the state championship!

There were several times when they were suppose to take some breaks in between, rest and get some relaxation, but instead they decided to hang out with the basketball team and did things they weren't suppose to do. Well if they were taking the breaks they were suppose to they would have been rested for their basketball practice the very next day!

You have to pay attention to what is going on in your life, and in the lives of those around you. Always take time, take a break, show your family some love the best way you know you can. There is nothing wrong with giving them a shout out every so often. You just never know how you giving them your time, and taking a break from all the irons that you have in the fire could be a game changer. Showing your kindness could mean the world to them. Just sometimes you have to push back from your grind, and help someone else with their daily grind. Well you know what that does when you share your wealth, it is multiplied back into you!

Give, and it will be given to you. They will pour into your lap a good measure—pressed down, shaken together, and running over [with no space left for more]. For with the standard of measurement you use [when you do good to others], it will be measured to you in return." Luke 6:38 Amp.

When you give you aren't giving as unto men, but you are doing it as unto the Lord!

Whatever you do [whatever your task may be], work from the soul [that is, put in your very best effort], as [something done] for the Lord and not for men, Colossians 3:23 Amp.

Yes take your breaks, even a mini break sometimes even a mini break will do. You know what they say about power naps will do for you! Sometimes a power nap in between work, and chores, and things to do at home could be the very thing that you need to do! You may not be able to get in a full hour, but perhaps a fifteen to twenty minute power nap may be what you are looking for. Sometimes you may not have the time that you think you need to do something, but make the time to take a break, and it really will help to get going the next day!

Sometimes your intentions may be something of which you endeavor to clean the bathroom, do laundry, go to gym, as well as a myriad of other things. However, in all actuality when you get home, you go to asleep! Well perhaps that is exactly what you need to do. You don't always have to ask for permission either. Just lay down, and take a nap.

If the little's are running around see if he'll watch them for a bit, while you curl up, and get some me time in! Don't do something just because you see everyone else doing it. If you see a post, and everyone says when they get home, they do this, and that, well more power to them. You have to do you, and what works for you!

Do what suits you. If others are asking you to do something, and you aren't feeling it then don't do it. It's that simple. If they asking you to be apart of something of which you don't want to do then why bother. King Saul was trying to give some of his armor to David so he could fight Goliath. For some reason he just felt like that suit of armor wasn't for him, so he really didn't even consider putting it on.

Instead David took five smooth stones, and proceeded to go after his Goliath, even though people were afraid, and they didn't even want to deal with him.

What are some of the things that you don't want to deal with? What are some of the things that you think is too much work? Your answers will tell you what you may be struggling with without even knowing it!

There are some things that aren't necessarily my favorite thing to do initially. However when I get started, and get moving toward those things in life it does get easier. Some of the things that I don't care for are pulling weeds, cleaning the fridge just to name a few.

What I have learned to do over time is to just take breaks during the things that need to be done, but that aren't necessarily all that fun to do. When you do take periodic breaks it helps to keep pushing forward. It is also good to be sure, and eat, and hydrate!

Taking care of yourself A.K.A. as self-care is important in the day, and age that you live in! Now you don't want to celebrate your victories too soon now. Always do things in moderation, and you will always come out on top!

There is something to be said about doing things in moderation! Doing things a little bit at a time helps to ensure that you aren't getting ahead of the Lord! Always stay in line, and in step with Him, and when you continuously do this you can't go wrong!

Being in line, and in step means you may have some breaks, and there may be times to celebrate! There is a difference between celebrating, and having a quick laugh. Having a quick laugh doesn't mean that you just lay out in it. It may be as simple as watching a few Tick Toks, and getting a good wholesome laugh, and to keep it moving in the process of it all!

There is something to be said about keeping things moving! Whatever the Lord has put on your plate to do, or even on your platter be sure, and do every single thing that He has called you to do!

It could be something that may seem mynute, or it could be huge, and colossal. However, don't get your eye on something that could be huge, and colossal. The Lord will get you there whether it is huge or small.

Work with the smaller things until He gives you the bigger things. If there is a time period to where it seemed like the Lord was giving you the bigger things in life, and then some of the smaller things in life show up then perhaps it is a testing of your humbleness that He needs to look at.

Don't be so heavenly minded that you aren't any earthly good. There is nothing wrong with continually giving yourself to humble tasks, helping someone out with a ride. Doing errands for them, grocery shopping for someone, cutting someone's lawn, giving someone money to put in their gas tank, walking someone's dog, and a myriad of other things.

I had recently watched this movie called "Good Deeds," with Tyler Perry, and he helps out this single mother with buying her, and her child some food, as well as other things. Well it could be viewed as being a total waste of time, however if you do it as unto the Lord then nothing is a waste of time. The Lord uses everything! It is usually in those humble moments when you take your eyes off of yourself to help someone else that your character is built, and you start coming into your own!

When your character is being built it is going to take a lot more than what you may be thinking! The Lord likes to break things down, first look at what is working, and what is not! Just like a mechanic that works on a car, and takes things apart, finds out what is working, what is not and changed it out! Sometimes a mechanic has to order some parts, and it could take some time for those parts to come. Sometimes those parts are on back order, and sometimes those parts you have to shop around for them.

Either way just know that there is a season for everything. If things aren't happening quite as quick as you would like, then perhaps it isn't quite time, and the Lord is working on your set ups. When you are taking your rest periods, and taking your breaks be sure, and stay woke in the spirit, and to stay ready so you don't have to go around, and try and get ready!

Stay ready for your breakthrough, stay ready for your open windows, stay ready for your open doors, stay ready for your miracles, for your blessings are at hand!

Time To Reflect

1. What are some of the ways that you could take breaks throughout your day?

Time To Reflect

2. When you know even NASCAR drivers have pit stops, how can you pump your own breaks, and get that break in?

Chapter 6

Know Your Why

Sometimes you have to remind yourself why you do what you do. You have to remember why you roll out of bed way early in the morning before the rest of the house gets up!

You have to remind yourself why you do loads of laundry the night before in order to prepare for the next day! You have to remind yourself why you cook, and clean every single day for your family without skipping a beat!

You have to remind yourself of the joy of having to change so many diapers because it is a true blessing to have, and enjoy a baby! Having to do the dishes just means that you, and your family are eating well!

There are many families that are coming together, but they have strife, contention, and have jealousy of one another. Everything seems to be fine, but once you pull out further, and farther then where they were at all of a sudden people, yes even those in your very family appear to have a problem with the goodness of God that is so evident in your life!

They might give you tags like "well who does she think she is," or "she thinks she is so bougie," "she think she is so high, and mighty." I had a teacher tell me when I was working on my counseling in psychology degree “you have lofty goals.”

Well I thought I was suppose to, but she had made it sound like having lofty goals was out of the question. Maybe from where she was sitting it seemed farfetched, but I was young, and just getting started! If you have a teacher, or have had a teacher that is or has made comments of this nature, just disregard, and keep on moving!

That could be used of the enemy as a distraction to what you are working towards. Don’t let that let you get off track. A good way to stay on track is to know why you started, and wanted to do something in the first place!

Why do you want to go back to college to get a degree? Why do you want to have five children instead of two? Why do you want to have a family? Why did you want to have children? Why do you want to change your degrees?

Why do you want more pay on your job? Why do you want to be promoted? Why do you want to do what you want to do? It is important for you to know the reason behind why you want to do what you want to do?

It could get easy to get lost in all the “to do lists,” in all the loads, and loads of laundry, get immersed in all the daily tasks that you do on a regular basis!

You may want to ask yourself the question why you are getting so immersed in what your doing, not getting enough sleep, not having time to yourself to even eat, and are grumpy towards the other people that you love!

There may be some adjustments that need to be made along the way because it could also be the simplicity of managing your time better. When you manage your time better you are able to ultimately get more stuff done.

Changing the way you go about a day, and prepare for it the night before could be a total game changer for you. Yes, initially changes may seem difficult, or even arduous at times but it is okay because the Lord is going to want you to grow, and make changes, and adjustments along the way!

Those changes may include some of the things that you may enjoy, and also things that you may not enjoy as much. If the Lord has you do things that may not seem palatable at first He will eventually give you the grace to do those things that you would rather not do!

Doing those things that you may not like to do initially will help you to grow, and expand in ways of which you may not have been able to do so if you were able to do what you wanted, when you wanted, and how you wanted twenty-four seven.

Too many people nowadays only want to do the fun stuff without putting in the work, and doing what they need to do in order to rise to the top. Too many people want to have a job, but don't want to do the work, want to have a job, and not have to get their hands dirty! Want to have the benefits of the job, but don't want to do what is required let alone not even try to fulfill the job description!

That seems to be the order of the day nowadays where someone wants something for nothing. It really doesn't work that way! The reality is to work in some form for what you want, and then you will be rewarded accordingly!

What you may need to do in order for your breakthrough to come through may not necessarily be something that you would expect! Nonetheless the Lord knows what you need, and when you need it! He may still have some things that He needs to work in you, and through you!

When you have a ministry of any size there are going to be things that the Lord needs to bring out of you, and it may not come forth in the usual manner as it had always done in the past! Just know that the Lord knows exactly what He is doing, and that you need not hesitate not one bit in reference to whatever He chooses to do in your life, and when.

Perhaps the Lord has given you a huge vision for your ministry, and you know there is always provision for the vision! However the provision may come to you in increments, or little by little.

The Lord knows what may be trying to come down your path, so He may choose to hold some things up to allow those other things that weren't so optimal for you, and your family to pass! You may not understand fully what is going on verbatim, but nonetheless the Lord will begin to release those things in you as He deems to do so.

You cannot rush the will of God for you life, it just simply doesn't work like that! He will give you the direction for what you need at the moment, and will be able to give you further instruction as He aligns things ever so perfectly!

He may be fine tuning the whys that you have for your ministry, and may be widening the overall arching scope of everything! When you have ministry brewing within you then you already know that you are going to be fully equipped for everything that you could possibly need whether you have everything that you think you need or not!

Once you have realized that, and have started to walk in, and even own what the Lord has so graciously bestowed upon you, you will find that blessings will begin to seek you out, and that the tables of adversity have truly been turned!

Since the Lord works everything out for the good then you know that whatever had been held up before, will begin to trickle down, and begin to manifest!

Perhaps there are even more new discoveries for you and your emerging, and budding ministry that may still remain to be seen. Take your time with these new discoveries, and don't be in such a hurry to move onto the next phase.

The next phase will come in due time. You really don't want anything that is out of your due time, or out of your due season!

Let us not grow weary or become discouraged in doing good, for at the proper time we will reap, if we do not give in. Galatians 6:9 Amp.

There is a due season, or a proper time for you to come into your own (sort of speak). However you must wait on that due, and proper season. When you wait like that you know that good things will come to those that wait!

Waiting on the Lord with a proper attitude, and disposition will allow you to stay in complete alignment with Him. Knowing your why will help you to continue to go with His flow, and not get off into something else.

That means you have to continually rock it steady regardless of what is going on around you. The enemy likes to distract you so hopefully you won't get off of the faithful things that you had been doing all along that have to produce in your life!

When those things begin to hit, and come forth you'll be able to do more for the body of Christ, and abroad! Doing more for the body of Christ will in essence bring a satisfaction of which nothing could be compared to.

When you lean into doing such a thing, and aren't afraid of all of what the Lord has bestowed upon you it is then that you will embark on a whole notha level!

These are then levels in which others may want to acquire, but may not be able to achieve like you may have because you chose to go through all the obstacles, situations, and circumstances without doing all that grumbling, and complaining as many others tend to do when squeezed!

If you are one of those that it seems like you are being squeezed in some form or fashion don't let that bother you! It comes with the package, it will help you in the long run, and it is okay to be different.

You can't be like Christ if you are trying to be like the world! The world needs more people that will walk in their God given abilities, skills, and anointing! The world needs more people that aren't willing to compromise, and aren't willing to cower in the midst of adversity!

Adversity is the breeding ground, of which greatness is birthed forth. You just have to allow the process to continue, and to not flinch when all of this is being developed in you, and being forged forth! Greatness is what is being called forth in you, because that is exactly what is needed, and necessary for such a time as this! Don't rely on yourself, and rely on what you could do! If you do this then you are in essence being misled! When you are being lead by the Lord you could never go wrong!

When you follow the Lord's leading each, and every time then you will always be in line, and in step with the Lord, and that is exactly how you are going to want to have things.

Don't be afraid of the new newness that you may be coming into. The Lord rewards those that diligently seek Him on the daily.

Things will be more, and more apparent when you hang out with the Lord long enough! Hanging with the Lord means hanging with Him throughout all the different seasons in life, and not just the fun, and colorful seasons! That means staying with Him all throughout the other days as well.

The Lord never said that life was going to be rainbows, and tulips. He never said that you would be frolicking, and tiptoeing through the tulips! No, He never said that.

Consider it nothing but joy, my brothers and sisters, whenever you fall into various trials. James 1:2 Amp.

So when you have moments when you are going through, or working through something you are supposed to count it all joy! Granted it may seem easier said then done however it is doable!

Be assured that the testing of your faith [through experience] produces endurance [leading to spiritual maturity, and inner peace]. James 1:3 Amp.

Sometimes it is literally work to keep, and maintain your peace! That is something of which you don't ever want to give up, or forfeit! It is there where you will find your power, and be able to continue to make progress, and scale walls of which others wouldn't have been able to!

And let endurance have its perfect result and do a thorough work, so that you may be perfect and completely developed [in your faith], lacking in nothing. James 1:4 Amp.

Knowing your why will help you to keep going even though those times of testing can get a little testy! You have to stay out of the flesh, and ride it out in the spirit!

Therein you will find your victory! You cannot give way to the flesh, because it is there where the enemy is trying to take you so he could try to have some leverage. When you take it up in the spirit it is there that you will remain in victory because the enemy can't stand in the spirit so he has to rely on you acting out in the flesh!

Understand this, my beloved brothers and sisters. Let everyone be quick to hear [be a careful, thoughtful listener], slow to speak [a speaker of carefully chosen words and], slow to anger [patient, reflective, forgiving]; James 1:19 Amp.

When you make the habit of not being quick to respond to every little thing, and you make it a habit to quiet your insides you will no longer be in a place to where the enemy can trip you up with such simple fleshly things! So staying the spirit will ultimately help you to steer clear of such things!

When you have a vision so big on the inside you don't need much on the outside. You won't have to have five friends approval of a dream or vision the Lord hasn't given them! That reminds me of a movie "Leap" where Felicie had a dream of dancing ballet in Paris, but lived in a orphanage with her friend.

Well her friend had one good-sized postcard and she wanted to see it one more time, but they were both tugging on it, and it ripped in half! So she had a dream, and half of a postcard to go off of. They had somewhat of a plan A.

Felicie had one thing that was left with her at the orphanage when her mother had dropped her off! She carried it around with her like it was a million bucks! You have to pay attention to those people in your life that make you feel like a million bucks!

When you take the time to figure out those people that make you feel like a million bucks, or feel like sunshine on your face perhaps it is then when you find the why as to why you do what you do!

Sometimes when you are right smack in the middle of a daily grind, changing diapers, doing loads of laundry, doing all the dishes that are spread all across the sink, the sink counter, sprawled all throughout the house, in the middle of vacuuming, mopping, running errands, and answering your toddlers endless stream of questions feeling all pressured out take a moment look into their eyes and let them know that you hear them, you are there for them, and that you still remember the day when they came into the world.

Take the time to remind them of how special they are, and how much you need them in your life as much as they need you, and depend on them.

You are their center of gravity so you have to keep all those spinning plates in the air, and not let one of them drop. You might ask how are you suppose to do all of that, cook meals, clean up, grocery shop, pick them up from school, and do teachers conferences and the whole shabang?

Well, I'm glad you asked! Go to the one, and only that knows you better then you know yourself. Once you yes etch in that time, give Him time of day it is in those moments that He will show you the game plan, and show you how to run things, run things effectively, and come out on top! The daily grind doesn't have to be arduous. Pick your battles, and it is not with your toddler lol! In your moments with the Lord you will find everything you need to succeed!!

Time To Reflect

1. Why do you do what you do?

Time To Reflect

2. Once you figure out your why it will be easier to chart your course in life. What are you going to do different to keep the spinning plates in the air?

Chapter 7

Motivation Is Key

It is important to keep your motivation in check. I would even go as far to say that you need to protect your motivation!

When you protect your motivation, and do your best to continue to feed your motivation, and your drive then you wouldn't have moments to where you felt like your well of creativity has dried up.

It is so important to research some new ideas, and to go ahead, and build off from the older ideas. The Lord could use them both! If you find yourself in a place where you feel like your motivation is lacking, think about your why, think of ways to encourage yourself, and keep moving things forward.

That is one of my mottos is to keep things moving. If you could manage to keep things moving then in essence you are well on your way! Some may even wonder how you are able to do what you are doing, and how with everything going on in the world that you are able to stay on top.

Well when you strategize, change things around, and have different approaches to different situations, and circumstances you are not being predictable at all.

Throwing your own curb balls sometimes will also help to keep things popping! If you always have the same moves, the same response, the same approach to life, and are negative then your life will exemplify exactly that.

If you don't like what you are reaping then it is high time that you change what you are doing in some form or fashion, and see about changing things around so you could have an expected outcome!

There is absolutely nothing wrong with being able to receive everything that you had been believing for. You may wonder if you could have your cake, and eat it too! Well you can, but you are definitely are going to have to put in, and do the work! You will not be able to go to the next several levels unless you are able to roll up your sleeves, and do the work! What do you do when you feel like you need to be motivated?

Maybe there was something that was irritating you, and when that happens you hardy feel like doing much let alone kick some butt, and taking some names (sort of speak). Interesting enough when you are taking some new territory the enemy is going to want to come around, and take back some of the other old areas that you had conquered already!

When those moments try to come around, and pop up whatever that may be, steady your course. There has to be an ultimate reason as to why it seems and it appears like everything is hitting the fan!

Well don't be easily fooled by what you may be looking at, and what may be trying to dance in front of your face. You have to remember what your why is, and then once you narrow that down, then you could go ahead, get a game plan, jot some things down, and revert back to what you had jotted down when those moments try to come and eat your lunch!

The whole point to that is to get you to break your focus, and to get off of the direction in which you had been going for quite some time. You had been going in a certain direction for so long to where you know that you are getting ready to have a breakthrough!

Just like a woman that is in labor, getting ready to give birth and she starts to bear down and get ready to give birth. Either way you look at it, it is going to happen because once you get that threshold the baby is getting ready to come forth! Birth in, and of itself is something of which is going to take everything you got.

The process cannot be slowed down. It has already commenced, so it is just a matter of time for it to happen! It is time to celebrate when the baby is getting ready to come down the birthing canal. You usually prepare for the birth of the baby ahead of time by buying a crib, baby clothes, preparing a nursery, buying crib sheets, and whatnot.

You'll also get a boatload of diapers and things of that nature! You'll need to get some diaper wipes, and nail cutters, lotion, shampoo, and so forth. You'll most likely have a baby shower, and invite your family, and friends.

People will tell you not to celebrate too early because you don't want to jinx yourself or something like that. I would go ahead and say that you prepare for what you are believing for.

You also do celebrate somewhat because something new is getting ready to come forth, and it will change the trajectory of your life overall, and the life of those around you.

You will get a stroller, car seat, bassinet and anything else you could think of because once a mother is home with their baby they usually won't be frolicking, and playing out and about too much because you have to be careful around other people because you want to keep the baby healthy. Once the baby is born you'll have to take the baby for check ups, and the mother will need to be checked out too!

Perhaps some of the same things could be done with the things in the spirit. Make those preparations for all those dreams, and aspirations that seemed like they were taking forever to come to pass.

Make preparations for those things that you have been hoping, and believing for for so long! Have a mini celebration, and then when the blessed event comes, and a full manifestation starts to show up, then you could rejoice even more!

Think about those times when you had prayed for exactly what you had just received! Remember all those prayers that you had prayed, all those times you could have given up, think about those times when it seemed like everybody else's breakthrough was coming except for yours, think about all those that are still believing but haven't received yet, then go, and encourage them, and help to bring them along!

It is so much more of a reward when you are able to help someone else out, and to not always be thinking about yourself. The enemy would love for you to be all into yourself, be all into bringing your dreams to pass, be all into manifesting what you think is yours, and what you may think may be coming to you.

Have you ever heard of the term to spread the wealth? I have always had, and maintained the thought process to whatever the Lord would bless me with, or bestow upon me that I would always share the wealth!

I would not make it a habit to hoard things to myself. I have heard different people say that perhaps I would have a whole lot more money if I wouldn't give so much away. I give as the Lord leads me too, and He always knows exactly what I have need of. I would even go as far to say that He has the answers coming to me way before I even ask I just have to trust Him, and know that whatever I need is on the way!

I would also venture to say that instead of hanging out in doubt, and in fear, I do my best to do otherwise. I cannot afford the thought process of thinking, pondering, or wondering if my Lord will come through because He always has, and He always will!

That is what you call relationship. You just learn to trust, and if it is something that I quite don't understand or it hasn't been revealed to me for some reason then to fill in that gap I just choose to trust, and stay in faith!

If you could ever get to the place to where you could just trust the Lord regardless of how the way things look then my friend you are way ahead the game!

Most people would have tapped out, but you have already made up in your mind that you are going to get whatever the Lord has put on the table for you, and that you will not get up from that table until you get everything that the Lord has put aside for you!

You may want everything right upfront, but it may not work like that. The Lord may release it to you little by little. Then once you do well with that perhaps the Lord will increase the dispensation, and may even up the ante because you have kept a good attitude for so long.

If you think about it when you are able to wait as long as you have been able to wait, just maybe all that patience that is being built in you will help to play out, and will ultimately help you to hone your new skill set that will take you over, and beyond your new threshold of blessings that the Lord is brining forth.

I'm sure you have heard the easier things in life don't take much time. Well the same thing goes for things that take a little more time. Those things are usually the bigger things in life. You have to learn just how to quietly sit, quiet your spirit, not have a response for every little thing, and keep, and maintain your composure.

When the enemy comes around it is to try, and rattle your cage. One might wonder why would he try to rattle your cage? Well perhaps it is to get you discouraged, to get you off track, and for your to get off of what you had been believing for.

Once you are able to overcome all of that, look for ways to be a blessing, look for ways to get out of your comfort zone, look for those open doors, and opportunities, look for ways to branch out in your ministry, look for ways that people have a need, look for ways that the Lord has shown up in your life before!

Sometimes when you take the time to reflect on the goodness of God, reflect on the different, various way He has shown up previously, reflect on how far He has taken you, reflect on where you had first began, reflect on the horizon ahead then you will most definitely find some more motivation. Write down all the different things that have motivated you before, and then apply it to your life accordingly!

It is then that guy will see the goodness of shod being revealed in your life over, and over again! You will begin to understand the meaning behind the song "Waymaker," and the lyrics that are associated with the song.

Just because you don't see Him working doesn't mean that He isn't, just because you don't feel Him working doesn't mean that the Lord isn't working diligently on your behalf! Release your mind, free your mind of the worry, and begin to truly believe the Lord for His best in your life, and watch it come to pass!

Time To Reflect

1. What are some of the things that helps you to stay motivated?

Time To Reflect

2. What are some of the things that you could do when you don't feel motivated?

Chapter 8

The Daily Grind

Your daily grind may be different then somebody else's! However, everyone has some type of everyday grind that may consists of To Do Lists, business meetings, planners, budget planners, calendars, conferences, Zoom meetings. Sales calls, client meetings, chores, play dates, and so forth. Wherever you may find yourself today learn to love the grind that you are in.

Chances are there are many people that are admiring you, and what you do. Truth be told they may even enjoy the life that you are now living. Never allow yourself to get to a place to where you regret the life that you had originally prayed for.

It is just that when you started to lay up all those prayers you actually had no idea all of what you were asking for would entail, and require! Once you get to the other side of what you had been believing for all along it is a whole notha world, and a whole notha level!

The reality of those prayers start to play out in your life, and you begin to realize that this was what all the fuss was all about. It begins to dawn on you! Things begin to make more since, and why you had to wait so long!

After all, you don't want anything that is half baked, or half done do you? You don't want anything that is before it's time right? I don't want anything that is before its time, after its time, or out of step with the Lord!

When you receive something from the Lord, and it is in line, and in step with Him things go smoother, there is no struggle, you don't have to push, you don't have to make it happen, you don't have to force anything!

All you have to do is to lean into what the Lord is doing for you, and through you, and follow through with every single thing that He has you doing. When you open yourself up to continue to be willing, and obedient then it will open things up for you on an even greater plain, and a greater horizon!

If you are willing and obedient, You shall eat the best of the land; Isaiah 1:19 Amp.

The Lord's word says that you will eat the best of the land, and not the worst! Sometimes the land that you may be looking at may not look like that at all! Just know the Lord Himself could literally change those tables altogether, and flip it in a whole new direction in your favor!

When those changes begin to come be sure, and lean into it! When you lean into the very things that the Lord is doing in your life, not living in fear, not allowing the enemy to rattle your cage, not allowing the doubt in your life to enter in, not listening to what the naysayers are saying around you, not paying attention to those distractions, not succumbing to what others may be doing or not doing when they aren't called of the Lord like you are, not getting off track when others are getting off track, not behaving as those behave in the flesh, not acting out in the flesh, but instead riding high in the spirit you then cannot be stopped!

You are the only one that could get in your own way! I know you don't want to get in your own way. I know I want to keep making progress even though I may not readily be able to see everything manifest that I would like to right away.

The everyday grind will sometimes have some type of switch up. Well whatever it is be sure, and be readily, and adjust accordingly!

There is no reason to get all bothered by it. Just trust that everything will work itself out, and you will soon be back on track, and making some progress like you always do.

Adjustment is apart of life. Just stay calm, adjust and carry on. Keep it moving. You don't have to get all in your feels. No, you don't have to do all of that. On the contrary, when you learn how to work through things without succumbing to your feelings then you are well on your way to the next chapter in your life! Don't be in such a rush to turn your own pages!

Allow the Lord to turn your pages, and ultimately turn the chapters in your book! He knows in which chapter you are supposed to be in for your life! If it is a chapter that you don't care to be in then by all means just roll with it. Learn to learn all the lessons that need to be learned.

I mention this because if there is a lesson that hasn't been learned then that same lesson will come back around again! I don't want to take any more tests then what I absolutely have to.

I just make it a habit to go along with whatever the Lord is wanting me to do, and He always brings me over to the other side to victory! Victory is what the Lord wants for you, and I!

He wants you to enjoy the experience of winning, and the experience of accomplishing something of which you had originally set your mind to do!

Set your mind and keep focused habitually on the things above [the heavenly things], not on things that are on the earth [which have only temporal value]. Colossians 3:2 Amp.

When you set your mind on things that are above, then you won't be so easily moved by the things of the flesh! Having a mindset that thinks about the things of God, more then the things of this world could be very freeing in, and of itself!

After all, with all this social media, all the not so good news on the television broadcasts, and all the different venues that pump different, and various information it could get quite confusing as to what is going on in the world!

It is so important to put some time in with the Lord first, and giving Him first dibs! After all, He waits for you to reach out to Him. Reaching out to the Lord, and knowing from hence where your help comes from will help you a great deal down the road. When others are going to their five friends, or when others go to the social media sources for answers, when others go to different counselors, and whatnot be sure and keep your trust in the Lord!

Trust in and rely confidently on the Lord with all your heart And do not rely on your own insight or understanding. Proverbs 3:5 Amp.

The daily grind is what you make of it. Go at it with all you got, ask the Lord to strengthen you daily for the journey, and watch Him begin to unfold the very things of your life like a tapestry of love of which He desires to help you with your day to day!

You are not alone, and He is always with you! Be encouraged, be uplifted, and keep standing up to the plate, and knocking it out the park each, and every day! In doing so you are leaving a legacy of the Lord's goodness to be enjoyed in your daily life!

Time To Reflect

1. What does your daily grind consist of?

Time To Reflect

2.What can you do on the daily so the grind doesn't become arduous to you?

Takeaway

When you determine, or set out to daily spend time with the Lord, put Him first in everything, and take Him with you on your journey the trajectory of your life is about to change! I'm not saying it is going to be tulips, and rainbows. What I am saying is the Lord will be with you every step of the way, and will help you to navigate through life successfully!

Made in the USA
Columbia, SC
06 May 2025

57578752R00054